PRIMARY READERS
PRE-MOVERS

Ozzie and Summer Sun

Marla Bentley
Illustrator: Matt Ward
Cover: Avi

Ozzie walks far.
He walks to the south.
It gets warmer and warmer
and he sees many different things.

Summer Sun is playing on the Equator.

Ozzie takes care of his friends. Every day they are weaker.

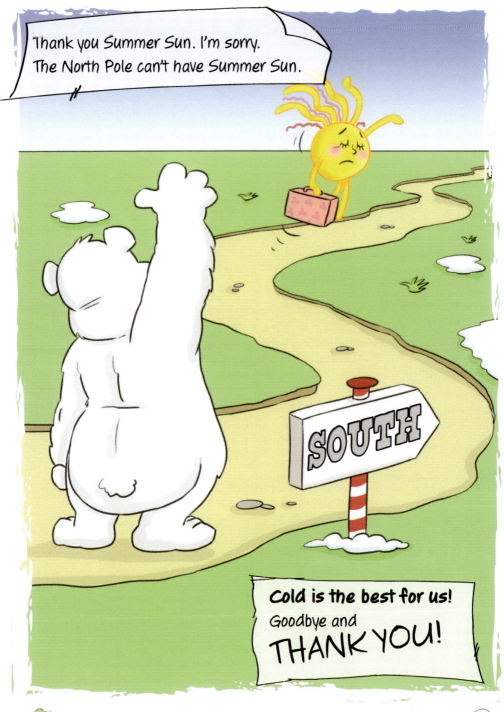

Picture Dictionary

23

Picture Dictionary

seal   snow   swim

walrus   windsurf   worried

strong   weak